understories

understories

POEMS BY Elizabeth Greene

Inanna Poetry & Fiction Series

INANNA Publications and Education Inc.
Toronto, Canada

Canada Council **Conseil des Arts**
for the Arts du Canada

 ONTARIO ARTS COUNCIL
CONSEIL DES ARTS DE L'ONTARIO
50 YEARS OF ONTARIO GOVERNMENT SUPPORT OF THE ARTS
50 ANS DE SOUTIEN DU GOUVERNEMENT DE L'ONTARIO AUX ARTS

The publisher gratefully acknowledges the support of the Canada Council for the Arts and the Ontario Arts Council for its publishing program, and the financial assistance of the Government of Canada through the Canada Book Fund.

The publisher is also grateful for the kind support received from an Anonymous Fund at The Calgary Foundation. CALGARY
FOUNDATION

Front cover photograph: Alan Clark

Cover design: Val Fullard

Library and Archives Canada Cataloguing in Publication

Greene, Elizabeth, 1943–, author
        Understories : poems / by Elizabeth Greene.

(Inanna poetry & fiction series)
ISBN 978-1-77133-150-0 (pbk.)

        I. Title. II. Series: Inanna poetry and fiction series

PS8563.R41737U53 2014   C811'.54   C2014-902113-5

Printed and bound in Canada

Inanna Publications and Education Inc.
210 Founders College, York University
4700 Keele Street, Toronto, Ontario M3J 1P3 Canada
Telephone: (416) 736-5356 Fax (416) 736-5765
Email: inanna.publications@inanna.ca Website: www.inanna.ca

For the memory of my mother
Hannah Shor Greene (1907-1980)
Queen of understories

Contents

Going the Distance for Poetry

Lost Cities

What I Like About Poetry

It says, *I prefer not to.*
It doesn't persuade, exhort,
encourage, scold or ask for
money. It doesn't say, *YOU can help.*
It doesn't tell you to lose weight,
try botox or Viagra. It doesn't say
have a good day.

Prickly, seductive, lyric, abrasive,
there's the poem. Read it or not,
like it or not, it shrugs, persists.
It doesn't promise white teeth or
true love. You can enter or you can
walk away.

One Perfect Afternoon

How have the arcs crossed?
How have the paths met?

—H.D., *Helen in Egypt*

One Perfect Afternoon

You arrived
looking like a 21st century Rembrandt
white shirt, tousled hair,
eyes full of mysteries, jokes, wild dreams—
some of them had actually come true.

We walked by the water, sat, talked
as if we did this all the time.
You took my hand.
Energies of the universe
flowed over us,
wind blew round us.

We dined with friends,
your leg against mine.
Perfect party, laughter, trout,
as if we'd always been here, at the centre
of this new-gathered group.

That night we kissed good-by
as if we'd meet again tomorrow.
You drove home in darkness; I flew
a thousand miles before dawn.

One perfect afternoon—do you remember?
We've scarcely spoken since.
You sent me one-line emails

as if you thought happiness a mere parenthesis,
as if your best work could only grow in suffering.

My friend says, one perfect afternoon
in twelve years is not enough,
Try internet dating, she suggests,
Don't waste your life in loneliness.

Splitting the Moment

3:37 a.m.
November darkness
only the stove clock glowing.
Outside the Leonids
trembling, falling,
bright sparks dropped
from a celestial spoon.
Inside, tortoiseshell Binah purring,
triumphant that the door opened
to let her in
without her even asking.
Shekinah pounces on my toes,
mouse practice. This moment
includes *claws*.

The moment's real story:
failure of nerve. I'm still scared
to go out alone at night even
for one of heaven's best shows.

It's not till nearly six that I
pad outside, yearn up toward
the fixed stars, the dippers
spangled overhead.

I'll get other wishes,
but none on these new moon Leonids.

Binah roamed half the night
under shooting stars. No wonder
she came home to such contented sleep.

I Know from Dreams

I know from dreams how it would be to lose my mind.
Giving parties where the wine glasses vanished.
Running for trains that left ten minutes before.
Time and space collapsing like absurdist spoons.
Just this morning I was driving people to a store ten miles from here
and had to come back home to get a present and a card
for someone's birthday. When I got out of the car, it was snowing.
I was in a bathing suit, clutching a flimsy coverall, feeling the snow
bite my skin, flake by flake. I got the coverall on in spite of wind.

Back home, I listened to the weather: lightning all over Canada at noon.
I could see the forks spreading across the weather map like migraines.
I petted the cats, got to the party without card or present.
The hostess came over, apologized she didn't
know my name. I said, *I was invited.* Then realized I didn't know her name
either. I was going to give her a book, but it had somehow slithered away.

I woke to an ordinary Thursday, gently purring cats, snow falling
not blowing. No bathing suits, no circuitous routes.
I managed to put my clothes on right side out,
not back to front or inside out, like
sometimes, even when I'm awake.
Starting the day, I push aside the thought:
dream may become the norm in twenty years.

Per Aspera ad Astra

When I first saw Saul Steinberg's cartoon,
his roadmap *per aspera ad astra*
I thought it travel enough
for a lifetime. Even in my teens
I understood the easy journey between Lex,
Pax, Lux, Pulchram, Sanitas—fifteen minutes,
half an hour's drive over straight roads
starting from Prosperitas, the norm in 1958.
Once bitten by divine discontent, seekers
leave all that behind, trek north, over roads
increasingly remote, uncertain, whited out
with sand or snow.
                              Caritas is close
enough, the road still paved and straight.
The next town, Labor, sits by a lake or bog,
a detour, as is Amor, on an island—
that's where we met—you working—
I lost, derailed, enswamped.

You were scared—love *is* a byway—Astra far off
and farther to the East. The road twists insanely
through Mediocritas—no one wants to stay there, but
it's on the way, more loops and curves, through Veritas, Timor Dei—
we've both known those—both spent time in remote Aspera.

Why didn't you take my hand—travel with me
footsore in our dusty boots?
We might have found that unmarked path to Astra.
You're miles away, and I don't know if I can reach
those far stars on my own.

Christmas Cards in January

It's definitely time to take them down
now that the dark of winter's giving way to sober
January light. The wine-red amaryllis fading,
trumpet petals thin as Jackie Kennedy's skin
the months before she died.

I love this pretty hodge-podge of good will
each card with its stillness
tying me by an unseen golden skein
to friends from Scotland, California, Vancouver Island.
Present back through years, frail
barques of friendship, far relations,
network of affection.

I love the pictures—snow-laden fir
picking up her skirts and entering the ball.
Owl, peaceful yet mindful in the snow-flecked air,
photographs of the first unblemished snow,
winter frozen without biting wind or slippery steps.

The cards say, Janus still looks back.
The New Year won't begin until I take them down.

Old Photographs

Spread round the living room,
here's Peri, her red-tailed hawk,
Meerak, on her curving arm.
Years later, Peri still walks her land
each day, lives its rhythms, greets the birds,
knows every tree, shows her grandkids
wildflowers and stars.

Here are two of Diane's horses:
grey Elke with her first foal
long-legged Leif. Much-loved Elke,
mother of champions, found last weekend
in pool of blood, brain aneurysm,
nothing to be done but mourn.
No photograph could tell that future.

Here's Gilda at her Toronto Golf Club wedding,
golden, cherished. She lives in England now,
bringing up her daughter and her son.

Here's Alan, making his stiff camera face,
at seven, ten, sixteen,
the mostly unseen eye,

snatching new-sprung mushrooms,
the white shimmer of iris after rain,
tulips ballooning red, yellow, purple every spring,
the real story behind the pictures:
his growth, his gift unfolding
struggle by struggle,
click by click,
frame by frame.

The Limitations of Photography

I love to look at photographs,
though most are fictions—
separating the moment
from the flow of time.
The photographer's eye
chooses what the lens records.

This one of us,
your back garden, 1994.
I'm trying not to throw my arms
around you. The photographs don't catch
your quicksilver imagination, your leaps
toward the world of angels,
your voice so polished
grocery lists sound Shakespearean.

But this picture does catch truth:
the distance between us,
unbridgeable,
prophetic.

Disturbing the Universe

Do I dare/ Disturb the universe?
—T. S. Eliot, "The Love Song of J. Alfred Prufrock"

Panic at the party,
all those assured, animated people—
I can no more speak
than plunge off a cliff. I gulp,
imagine I'm a hedgehog
bristling silence,

watch but don't talk,
try to become invisible.

All planets below the horizon
in my horoscope suggest
a complex inner life
that risks
staying shut as a clam.

When I'm with a friend or cat,
I uncurl
like a Chinese water flower,
find my voice,
know if I want, I can
disturb the universe.

The Language of Rivers

I

I want to learn the language of rivers,
the secret of their movement ever on

like a tune played on Andean pipes and bells
beginning in the hills, ending far off

ankle-deep with skittering bugs,
frogs, slithering snakes.

II

My river source:
the earth's molten core

cooling to blood and lymph

green my hands,
blue my feet.

III

August morning at the Crowe,
a river to wash off sorrows.

I sit in tiny waterfalls and feel the
push, plunge my ears under,
hear the bubble and plash, rush and lap,
the sounds beneath the surface
surreal as shadows:
blbblbbblbb
air whirled into water

Nothing matters here but the urgency
Of water and current.

Further down, deeper,
shadow patterns swaying,
clear brown golden.

The river says:
learn through immersion.

Heaven in Bits

Is it aging? Knowing there never
will be enough time? You need to be
thankful for what you've got.
Full moon flickering through clouds, misty, silver, gone—
sun transforming red bee balm and purple catmint
into a summer morning's spiky lights.

An hour in a Pre-Columbian museum in Santiago—
so many rooms and sculptures—
though from that too short time I still remember round, brown
clay figures unswerving as centuries pass over them,
pots the red-brown of eclipse, serene as moons.

The spell of moments I don't want to leave:
an incantatory voice on a fading phone
for the last time—blurred words, distance
without arrival.

Horoscopes

I fell in love with your horoscope,
nestled into your Taurus moon,
melted at your first house
Venus and Mercury kissing—
translating into silvery wit,
someone loved of love, soaking it up
like an eggplant does oil.
I liked your sixth house Jupiter
in Sagittarius, lucky! Your
Mars in Virgo—getting what you want
through service.

Now I find I looked up the wrong year!
Our horoscopes don't match.
Your Sagittarius moon doesn't touch
my planets. Your Pluto-Venus-Jupiter
t-square suggests underworld descent.

All year my horoscopes are telling me
something's ending—must
or whatever's coming next won't begin.

After all this time
I've fallen out of love.
I don't like silence and
I don't like your horoscope.

One Thing I Love About H.D.

She had crush after crush,
affairs that ended badly,
even marriage—her husband
left her for the woman upstairs—
I love you; I desire l'autre.

At seventy-four she wrote
The reddest rose unfolds.
She burned incense to
Athene, Artemis, Sophia—
but most of all, Aphrodite.

H.D. claims, you can
love up to death's door—
requited or not—no shame—
it's still the real deal.

No healing without Aphrodite.
Maybe no poems either.

New Year's Day, 2013

The Christmas flowers drying now
like seventy-year-old womens' aging furs
flattened with years of wear
pelts far from forests
where they lived and grew.

Cynthia's alstroemeria
white petals falling
glyphs of loss.

Three weeks ago
I cast my mind a thousand miles away
saw you running wild, banging into tree trunks,
lost in winter woods.
I grabbed your wrists.
A red angel came,
then a white one.
They put you in a sleigh bed,
pulled you—not back toward
your room and home but on
toward the blank edge.
I wept, even though
you were in the care of angels.

You used to say, *Angels surround you*
but spelled it "angles"
like a lapwing leading strangers away
from its nest or the secret name.

Another day, a third, blue, angel
came to your bed's foot. Steadily
they proceeded, a nine days' journey.

The night you died, I saw your soul
in blue, green, silver, soaring, dipping,
the disease running through your body
left behind, curled on the floor.

The petals fall faster. Snow outside.
A New Year starts.
The days creep toward light.

Elegy

All those years of silence, distance, absence
were only practice for this silence,
distance, absence.

Functional Families

We will it so
      and so it is
            past all accident.

            —William Carlos Williams, "The Ivy Crown"

Functional Families

I

I didn't have one—
but wait—what about
holding my father's hand
when I was two, his telling me
the war was over?
What about suppers on the screen porch
in summer, tunneling in snow taller
than I stood in winter?
What about my parents making up
bedtime stories? Buying me
The Wizard of Oz when I was five
and reading it aloud the whole of my birthday.
I know from my cats,
functional families are when
there's no place you'd rather be,
even though there are
other places you need to go.

II

Put your mind in your body.
Be just as you are.
Cats embody yogic wisdom
purring unconditional love,
but not so unconditional

they don't claw my leg when they want food
or scratch the new-upholstered chair when
they want out or rattle the screen door
when they want in
Tortoiseshell Binah, pragmatic hunter,
and her daughter Shekinah, grey, apricot
and white, snuggly, fluffy, unexpectedly
fierce—they lick each other's faces,
curl up like commas together on my bed.

Only when Shekinah's daughter Juniper
came back from Toronto, age 2,
scared to death, dark pewter, large-eyed,
growling and hissing
hiding under the sofa
lurking on top of the piano
did I wish my cats could listen to reason.
She didn't remember her mother or grandmother.
They didn't remember her. They chased; she ran.
hid in my dresser's second drawer,
curled on my yoga clothes.
When not hissing, silent.
What happened in those years?

By now, she's found her voice,
demands, purrs, even smiles—
sometimes sleeps with Binah on the porch.
A home where everyone has a voice,
is usually happy—
that's the best I can do with what I've got.

Owls

One day, high in the eucalyptus,
the owl stared down
with huge golden eyes,
so intense we were glad we weren't voles.
It's very brown, said Maureen,
at first I thought it was a cat.
The owl, lesser horned, magellanic,
tufts on its head, koala-nosed beak,
barred feathers.
One owl: the birth of the soul.

The second owl appeared
on a branch over the road,
grey lifeless bunny in its talons.
Yuck—but an owl's got to eat
or it won't stay round, sharp-eyed.
Two owls: a wonder.

The third owl graced us
our last morning—larger, more shapely,
motherly, fearsome,
feather horns more distinct.
Three: pure vigilance.

Terry

When we met, Terry was a
man whose wife had died,
black velvet jacket hanging
lopsided to the left as if he was
uncomfortable in his skin.
That spring, he decided
he really was a woman,
started counseling,
advice on makeup, clothes,
came out at 79. The only woman
I'd ever known who'd been
a colonel in the British Army,
ridden horses in Africa.
As a woman, she wore swishy dresses,
lime green or ice blue, with frilly necks,
good with her curled white hair and vivid lips.
She'd sweep through her parties, glass in hand.
Terry's parties:
lots of booze, no children, grownups only
in that sixth floor condo with views of town and river
on three sides. In winter, a gas fire in the living room.
Always something lurid about Terry's parties:
an ex-nun, Mary, dressed to the nines;
a friend whose husband left her for another man;
a smarmy woman with her grown daughter who visited
the old and sick and got them to
change their wills in favour of the Humane Society.

After Terry died, her daughter Sue
gathered us in her memory one last time.
For once, there were children.
It wasn't the last chapter of *À la recherche,*
but maybe next to last.
True, there was something sad,
some papering over the cracks at this last of Terry's parties,
something not quite right.
Someone said, *Terry's real contribution*
was getting us all together.
But I think it was the way she lived
with courage and an iron will—you could see it in
her well-manicured strong hands—
and a belief friends are just important as family,
that it's possible to survive
dysfunction and live with brio in great clothes.

La règle du jeu

I hardly remembered it at all.
Well, the hunt, the country house,
Octave's revelation of his love.
I didn't see the underpinnings of
politics (de la Cheyniest part Jewish,
but the classiest act), or of tradition:
Marivaux, Beaumarchais, Molière,
the devoted sassy servant with a life
and a bad marriage of her own.
I was in love; my brain must have been
on vacation. I didn't say: *what règle?*
What jeu? Why is this your favourite?
We just agreed it was a masterpiece,
drove home, broke out the cognac, went to bed.

Twenty years single, I understand the games:
l'amour, la chasse, le masque
and the rule: *civility*
shattered by Schumacher's jealous shot.
The end of the weekend. Beyond the film,
the coming of war.

Of course my ex is there, at the end of the row.
Eighty now, he looks like a minor character
in an Old Norse saga, shrunk but fit, strong-willed,
brain in good working order.
I say hello, he nods.
Does he still feel because I left,
he didn't win? That there's one rule for art
another for life?

When Does Childhood End?

We were on the ferry to Nantucket
one summer afternoon.
I was four and bored.
I remember wind, foamy waves,
the ferry's white-plumed wake.
I sat in a corner, sang "Home on the Range"
over and over, waves of song I could fall into
and never drown.

I don't remember Nantucket,
the sea, sky, horizon,
only the endless ride.

Why didn't I pay more attention to my parents?
I should have tried to decipher who they were
when they were still healthy, happy.
I loved my home, but even then I longed for
some ideal western range, mystic island.

Two years later we went to Cape Cod again,
rented a nicer house. I learned to read
in the attic with rain falling on the roof.
I read my way to Oz.

That fall, we moved. Uprooted, I spent
decades trying to recapture that childhood ease.

Playing Cards

I My Mother's Solitaire

My mother used to play solitaire,
nerves jangling out her fingers, swinging
leg and tapping toes, as she dealt the cards,
a hope it would all turn out.
By then she was married, a mother,
living in a pale green apartment in New York,
with friends, museums, concerts, travel.
Sometimes even when you have a happy ending,
you find you still want more,
might search for promise in the cards.

II My Solitaire

I've played solitaire too, seven card, five card,
clock, Montana, played till they all turned out.
Then sick as if I'd gorged on marshmallow,
I'd throw the cards away—until the next time.
My grandfather gambled away three houses
(I'm sure with cards).
The breath of discovery when the cards come up—
and then you have to play them. Just one more deal
might be the one with luck, might
translate into happiness.

In my mother's last illness, over Christmas,
I sat on the couch where she'd sat, numb,
dealt cards on the small table,
The cards came out all tangled—I'd try again.
The cards were stubborn,
no matter how many times I dealt them.
Too many jacks in the wrong places.
My mother died in March.

III Tarot

The Waite deck! A world I'd always longed for—
I knew it when I saw it. Part Arthurian romance,
part stage set, gorgeous queens, imposing kings;
questing knights, colours clear as spring. I loved
the man juggling two pentacles inside a moebius
strip; the seven pentacles growing pumpkin-like
on a well-trained vine; the Moon, a dog and wolf
yipping between two towers.
I shivered at the scary swords, the hairy Devil,
storm-struck Tower. In the Empress
with her flowered gown and flowing hair,
I found a mother. In the High Priestess,
standing in her temple, book in hand,
I found a teacher.

Playing cards, the palest,
pasteboard echo, still the breath

of discovery as you turn them over.
With solitaire, bridge, poker, each deal
is a statement from the universe:
you are loved or you are not. You are
lucky. Or not. Tarot says, *The Fool
starts on her journey And not alone.*

Mean Mothers

The day before Mother's Day
pinkest petal time of year
apple blossom and magnolia
I pick up the book *Mean Mothers*
looking for answers. Don't find them.
My mother wasn't *mean*—critical—
passed on a pot of self-doubt
so black I'm still scrubbing.

She was sick, dismayed, depressed,
sterreless— without star or rudder— but
not mean.

What happened to her angels?
They got her through her mother's death,
her father's gambling,
hovered while she worked her way through college—
triumphed in spite of scarlet fever, eighteen root canals,
graduated *magna cum laude,* made friends, got jobs.

Now I want other answers:
when did she start to think that things could never change?
When did expectation turn to disappointment?
Her life felt grey except when she was travelling—
how could she not be mean?

Raindrops Lounging on Magnolia Buds

Thirty-three years later I regret
I never told my mother I was pregnant
until I turned up in New York in June
belly swelling with baby.
If I'd been a better daughter,
we could have oohed and aahed
over the baby's rhythmic kicks,
gentle explorations of his tiny world inside,
could have shopped for baby clothes.
We could have talked toys, picture books,
what I'd need for the nursery.

My mother used to say
The test of sanity is coping.
Why do I think of that now,
this soft grey April morning
raindrops lounging on magnolia buds,
scilla unfolding blue as faith,
cats purring in their peaceful sleeps.
Maybe now it's safe to venture out
uncensored. Maybe now, not frozen
with coping.

Pregnancy was scary enough
without dealing with her worry too.
My first pregnancy ended at twelve weeks
in blood and grief. I never told her,

afraid she'd say it was my fault
and maybe it was—riding in the well
of George's MGB over bumpy country roads

feeling sick. Nothing I could do—his six-foot son
couldn't fit in back, had to be taken home.
The baby didn't stay.

How would my mother know
about mothers and daughters and babies?
When she was pregnant,
her mother was long dead.
Her father said *never have children.*

My mother wished for a grandchild.
His birth brought her the purest joy—
true, she'd forgotten everything
about babies—and she worried: *the baby is too thin;*
too fat. But at the end, when she could
scarcely speak, sheer will formed the words:
is the baby all right?

The test of sanity is coping.
Where does neurosis eddy into madness?
Where do fear and anger cross the line,
enclose a mind with fog?
publicly, she coped—lined up her whole
apartment building to resist the owner's decision
to take it co-op—found good lawyers, stalled the deal

until the market sank and tenants could afford to buy their homes.
Privately, she worried when I went out the door at night,
was stiff with terror when I returned.
Don't buy a car, certainly not a house; don't get a cat, she warned,
as if stasis was the only safety.

Her love of art remained till her last months.
It's ravishing, she'd say—and when she
visited me in a dream after her death, she said,
her best self, *Isn't it beautiful?*

Now I see I didn't always cope,
didn't answer letters, return phone calls,
clean, dust, garden, wanted to throw dishes
at people who dismissed me as mere mother,
a struggling one at that. Threw words instead,
unforgiveable.

Now I wish I'd wrapped myself in light,
dispelled the fog.

My mother wouldn't like
this small house, this quiet street,
wouldn't understand demanding cats
who keep the house alive, their scratches, meows
images of all desire; their purrs echoes of the planet's hum.
She wouldn't understand why I'm besotted
with clumps of golden crocus in my front garden
or how I can sleep when my son's out till one or two.

If I wake up, I say, *did you have fun?* And when I'm out, he asks,
Did you have fun? When I say, *Yes,*
he answers, *Good.*

Summer's Children and Their Mother

1 Doris

This is Midnight. He's broken out of the barn.
He's running away. Doris, at 11, copper curls
half-combed, belt drooping under striped t-shirt,
looks at the horse she's painted, adding a last touch.
The photo's in the book *Summer's Children.*
Doris was always drawing and painting.
I still remember her horses and princesses,
stories to go with them.
She, her mother Rae, her younger sister Liz were family friends.
She and Liz the first girls I knew to leap from life
inside the pages of a book.
Liz was just drinking milk, but Doris' picture
announced her talent.
What would become of such a gifted artist?

What happened was, she had a breakdown at nineteen.
Then another. Kept painting, conjuring horses,
princesses, mountains into life.
The doctors thought she'd kill herself by thirty, but
she didn't. She had shows in New York.
My mother never took me.

I lost track of Doris long ago.
I know she was still living in New York

into her forties. I regret
I never saw what happened to her pictures.

II Rae

Their mother Rae had money but no beauty.
She was generous but nervous.
Never enjoyed her daughters' gifts or long-limbed grace,
packed them off to schools and camps.
Her pastime, worry.
Her passion, antiques—well-made chairs and tables,
cunning footstools, gleaming lamps.
She lived in their polished stillness
in her pale, high-ceilinged house.
Others were in storage, *all over the Eastern Seaboard,*
said her daughter Liz.

Rae had breakdowns too, electroshocks,
got better, got worse. In recovery, she was sharp-tongued,
which made me think niceness might be bad for health.

She faded from life in a hospital in Texas;
her daughters long-estranged.

Her antique glass-topped tables,
the chair she gave me, cat-scratched now,
stuffing spilling from the red and gold upholstery,
keep her with me, fragments of her afterlife.

III Liz

Good at crafts, athletic, Liz wasn't great at school—
how could she be with all that worry
and an unstable older sister?

When she was seventeen to my fourteen,
we forged a friendship. Later I was a junior counselor
at her camp. How competent she was away from home!
She sparkled—the director's right-hand woman.

Liz gave me survival skills:
Be independent, make your own appointments.
Mothers can't nag if you do it before they say.

Liz detested antiques, found them musty.
They made her think of the refrigerator
filled with mold and fur when she came home.
Mother never throws a thing away.
Her apartments were furnished modern;
her fridges clean.

Last I heard, Liz was living in Vermont,
married, a mother.
She carved out a quiet life, but still,
a life.

Grandpa Shor

He visited a few times when I was young,
a frail sad man, old in his sixties, white-haired,
long hands. From a long line of rabbis,
though I didn't know it then. My mother
looked like him, though I didn't see it then.

Twenty-five years before, his life had shattered.
His wife died, and his only son.
Absorbed in grief, he abandoned
his teenage daughters to make their own ways.

Now, visits without much warmth
to his elder daughter and only
grandchild playing on the rug,
watching, dazed, maybe afraid that death
would take me too at seven.

I unaware of those past tragedies,
not knowing what a grandparent might be,
saw only a man from the country of age,
half-withdrawn, slouching on the couch.

He died when I was nine. My mother cried,
went to Massachusetts for the funeral, left me
home, didn't speak of him for nearly thirty years.

Miracles

I thought miracles were supposed to be easy,
less work, more graceful,
gifts sudden as otters.

So here I am in the middle of a July night
hooked up to an intravenous drip,
sprouting machinery,

no longer a simple person—
it takes this array of tubes and monitors
for one to become two.

Everything's blurred
my glasses taken somewhere
with my clothes, my books.

I'm naked under my hospital gown
reduced to essentials
in this lurid light

the vestibule of afterlife.
I sleep between contractions
grabbing eternity where I can

The baby isn't coming,
seems headed for my spine,
mad as hell.

Daylight comes, and doctors.
One says, the baby's turned,
transverse.

I need to push so
he can be turned by hand.
I can't. I do.

Alan arcs into the world.
They take him, wash him,

stitch me up.
It doesn't feel
like a miracle.

But once I've slept,
much later,

maybe it does—
with Alan in my arms
delicate as a tiny seahorse,
unfurling.

Inheritance

Long before she died, the mother
who put me to bed, made up stories,
came running when I woke with
nightmares—wolves chasing at my heels,
dangling skeletons blocking my path—
had vanished into ripping criticism,
chilling scorn.

I've set up an interview;
don't think you'll get the job.

Then she was furious that I didn't go.

I didn't fulfill her life—
but then I didn't stay
a well-dressed doll, a fantasy,
no trouble.

What if she'd said: *you may not*
get the job, but you'll enjoy the meeting.
You can learn a lot, and you can always try again.
That was her unintended legacy to me.
I'd do it wrong, get tangled, try again.

Now, sitting at the Wolfe Island Bakery,
spending an hour with my son's photos,

dancing tulips, the reddest starlet roses,
opera singer orange lily, white irises.
I wonder if my mother would recognize
the mingling of her husband's talent,
her own unerring gift for perfect beauty.

Time Travel

True, it's just one way,
but even one way's a trip.
Memory is a kind of accomplishment
says William Carlos Williams.

I like to revisit former ages,
my childhood rooms with pictures,
dolls and books—

think of the games I played with marbles,
Rachel, Robin and a band of friends,
journeys far off, struggling home.

In my dreams I flew—or led an army of Indians
and dinosaurs against an evil enemy.

Where did the nightmares come from?
Skeletons and wolves in hot pursuit.
I'd wake screaming.

My parents never spoke their doubts and fears,
left me to guess the truths below the surface.

Today I travel through those layers of years,
take my past selves by the hand and bring them

finally, home—yellow walls, good light,
cats, books, a space where they can
draw birds, dream of unicorns.

Not my own child, but mother to my flock of selves.

Going the Distance for Poetry

How is it far if you think of it?

—Ezra Pound, Canto LXXIX

Going the Distance for Poetry

Two planes, taxi, two hour wait,
then bus to Muenster past golden canola fields
ducks in flooded ponds—*make sure they let you off
at the Shampoo Shack*—a short bumpy car ride along
a dusty road—
Why do I have to go so far to write a poem?
Muenster's not Parnassus,
the bus not exactly Pegasus.
It must be the leap of faith:
at journey's end
the veil will part; poems will appear.

This country, an hour east of Saskatoon,
all earth and air,
towering spruce trees planted long ago,
cones clustered at the top—
settlers leaving this gift of trees.

Brother Demetrius guides us past the cloister
into the chapel with its bright stained glass
wavy blue river from the Book of Revelations.
Silvery organ pipes cascade
on the back wall, tall to short,
three organs fused to one.

Returning from the abbey to the college,
we see a welcoming statue of St. Benedict

and his sister St. Scholastica.
Benedictines are rooted in the land,
says Brother Demetrius, stay in their
house for life—and after. The
peaceful cemetery edged by spruce
and cypress, the grey stone markers,
keep memories of monks alive,
living and dying in a stretch of earth
that care makes sacred.

First lessons in the language of trees:
the elm outside my window
with her three sisters
is teaching me to say
good morning to the sun
carries the rustle of rain
storm from the south
telling me the changes
sweeping across the prairies.
Leaves flutter in the wind,
whisper in sun, register
the patter of rain.

It's easy to awaken here,
with summer green,
brown dust roads,
browsing deer, crows screeching

warnings about strangers,
flittering goldfinches, butterflies—

northern lights—
great wall of a ghost cathedral
reaching above the pole.

Bells from St. Peter's steeple
ring high above the fields.

Leaping Over Fragments

Those bits of Sappho's poems that survived
twenty-five hundred years
disintegrating parchment—
Reading her's like walking
on wobbly stones through streams,
glimpses of girls flitting through distant copses.

Those tantalizing vanished words!
Those fragments!
Trying to clutch at dative plural endings
to find the sense—like grabbing at Peter Pan's
heels as he flies out the window, leaving
only his shadow.

So many poets have traveled here before
balancing the echoing gaps
against those sparse imperishable words.
How many have puzzled over *poikilothron*?
(Anne Carson says *spangled*).
All dazzled by the crowns of violets,
the rich gold bracelets, purple cloaks,
the golden mist of Aphrodite

making us want to know those girls
conjured with a name, a word—
lovely Atthis who left Sappho
for Andromeda,
shapely Mnasidike, melodious Gongyla,
and one, unnamed, blown into life by H.D.'s
weaving of Sappho's words:
I think no girl can ever stand beneath the sun
Or ever will again and be as wise as you are.

Last Week

Fifty years ago
the last week of Sylvia Plath's
writing life.

Six poems in three days:
The blood jet is poetry,
There is no stopping it.

Poems wrung from grey, cold
February, not-quite-furnished flat,
from squalls of toddlers,

from the shock of heart's emptiness,
her husband gone. The marriage behind.
The quest plot galloping

to its midwinter end.
Words dry and riderless—
her own soon to be orphaned.

The woman is perfected.
Her death rushing up
like waves breaking on shore.

Leaving Chile

How do you get to the spirit world?

In the air we see the salsa lights
of Santiago swirling under stars.

*

On my seatmate's screen
I see a young man with a wide crinkled smile—
Haitian, warm-skinned, loose-jointed.

Do you like it when they call you the Black Picasso?
Asks the interviewer in subtitles.

Not so much. It is flattering,
but it is also demeaning.

*

Crossing the equator:
distance traveled—2582 miles
distance to destination—2834 miles.
Good-by, finally, Andes.

How will we find poems
in the midst of dailiness?

*

He's Jean Michel Basquiat—
I'd vaguely heard of him
when I was deep in child-rearing—
twenty-five years later I'm starting to catch up.

His paintings, shamanic, the spirit world
sizzling on canvas—
died, August, 1988, age 27, heroin.
Burned up his life in painting.
Dead more than 20 years. I'll never know him better
than I do this minute, on this soundless film.

*

For Basquiat, heroin was the car,

heroin and ancestral knowing in his blood.

36,000 feet should be high enough,
but cramped and confined, I can't begin to reach
the heights Basquiat did on New York streets.

We arrive over Toronto, its straighter lights
welcoming, not dancing, in January dark,
touch down, speed billowing over the tarmac
before brakes rein us in.

Moments away from returning to our winter lives—
how to burn them into meaning?

Basquiat might say, *you can enter the spirit world
from where you are. Anywhere you stand can be the door*

Paterson Ewen

I hear his pictures speak.
The titles make it easier to leap
from glimpse, *augenblick,* to understanding.

"Precipitation": inexorable black drops
against a mustard-coloured sky.
Rain the morning of a promised picnic.

"Flying Rope": real rope against flat background,
the power of the spiral, like a gut.
I saw my insides once, pink and cave-like
on a screen. I recognize them in this thick hemp curve.

"Satan's Pit": a lighter mustard sun
gouged with lines, concentric circles,
black hole in the middle, bottomless,
made of steel, no light.
You're going step by step
through an eventless life and you fall in.
No instructions for getting out.
As below, so above—the psyche's black hole
in an indifferent sun.

The basic shapes:
suns, moons, spirals, dots
that could be rain or far dwarf stars.
Gouges in wood—the energy of water, sky,

even angry movement offers hope
like those climbing moons,
like balloons or lungs
around a spine,
climbing upward
answer to depression
or "Halley's Comet as seen by Giotto"—
clear blues and greens,
an eight-pointed star, smile on its face,
joy of the body streaks through outer space.

As below, so above.
as in the body, so in the heavens.
Moments of delight. More often,
heroic disappointment,
cosmic anger

Gulping Silence

after a painting by Marc Rothko

Sometimes I can't make sense of what I'm seeing—
like on the flight to Chile I saw mountains,
pure white jags and edges rising over clouds.
Were they really heaven-splitting Andes?
Or just majestic masses foreboding storms?

When I first saw the Rothko reproduction,
three rectangles—blue-black, pure blue, pure black,
I wrapped my soul around the blue,
but wondered why an artist would pour his lifeblood
into this particular form—though better puzzling form
than none at all.

Not the turquoise square of sunlit pool
edged with blue-green spiked agave and smiling daisies,
not the cerulean blue of Chilean sky
or meditative Adirondack peaks and valleys,
blue shading blue, mountains murmuring
ancient philosophies from time beyond memory.
Not the black of cool lake at night slipping over
summer-heated skin.

This painting gulps silence,
havens of pure colour in the scurrying world,
owls or angels hovering half-glimpsed behind the black.

Looking again I see the line
of cobalt blue around each edge
holding them all secure
in the certainty of eternity.

Still Life With Music

On my table with Sharon Olds'
new poem in the *New Yorker* about falling in love
all over again with her mother
are sheets of music, first time in fifty years.

I gave up singing, November, 1961,
scrunchy leaves, bare-branched trees
stretching toward winter. I'd been singing
"se Florindo è fedele, io m'inamoriro" week after week.
My teacher loving her own voice, bored with mine—
my lessons paid a smidgen of her rent.

I gave up singing, started studying.
By grad school I couldn't sing words, just notes,
my throat felt small as a dime.

Now I understand how hard that year was
my mother's brain tumour starting to manifest
as inexplicable anger. My first-year English teacher died.

On the far side of school,
my music on the table,
distant relative of cubist
paintings with violins and horns—
silence ready to burst into song.

Io ho sofferto molto

Io ho sofferto molto,
murmured the Italian artist,
his arms around me—
my cheek against his neck,
his well-shaped ear.
Opening my eyes
I could see a fringe
of dark blond hair.
As he kissed me
in an olive grove near
Fiesole I thought
I'd like to suffer too and
be an artist.
I didn't know then that
you can spin your wheels
suffering as in anything else.
It's practice
turning sand into pearl
over and over
makes the artist.

Divided Against Myself

When I'm in one of those moments where I'm pulled
two ways or more—how should I use my one and only
morning? I think of poets who were divided too,
made their limbo into poetry.

Yeats called it self and soul,
Owen Ahearne and Michael Robartes,
blood and the moon.

Sylvia Plath, who read Yeats,
called it wanting every fig at once,
but also the yellow of skin,
gold of moon, contradiction
of perfection to the messy changes:
bleeding, pregnancy, fretful babes.

Why shouldn't poetry grow from an itch
a quarrel, a divided self pushing
one opposite against another?
Despair against hope,
music against discord
time against eternity.

Opposites war against themselves,
but in poetry, they join hands,
lean back, spin
so there's nothing but
earth and sky
whirling into dizziness.

The Love Embrace of the Universe, the Earth (Mexico), Myself, Diego, and Señor Xolotì

Love's always a miracle
no matter how it twists and turns and bends
no matter that Diego beat his wife
or that she painted it
or that they both had other lovers.
Near the end of Frida's short life
this painting with the wisdom
born of a battered, much-loved body
a life of struggle to arrive
at this serenity: Frida in red,
a wide Madonna skirt,
Diego, as a baby, in her lap,
his third eye wide open.
Both in the embrace of Cituacoatl,
Aztec Earth Mother, made of clay and rock
all in the embrace of the half-visible goddess sky.
The painting's a meeting of leaf and root,
earth and sky, sun and moon.
Just below Frida's flowing hem,
her small gray itzcuintli dog, Señor Xolotì,
sleeps, curled,
guide to the underworld,
whom Frida will follow in five years,
Diego, eight, while the painting
hangs on the wall, draws us in.

Vibration

The simplest way to soar
to outer space. If I sing "Skye Boat Song"
or you play Mozart's "Sonata in C Major,"
we're already half in another world,
with its own time, language, rules.

In the gym turned concert hall,
gongs are attuned to New Moon,
Full, Mercury, Venus, Mars, Saturn, Pluto.
Struck, they throw circles of sound
to our cores, affirm
we are linked to everything on earth
through heavens.

I thought the music of the spheres would be
brighter, more like Scarlatti,
less like Beethoven's growly underside.
But when David Hickey plays those gongs,
I hear planets' crashing energies,
immensities of space between stars.

We stumble into the night, dazed by vibration.
The full moon whitens the blossoms, glitters
the water, sends out its song, expecting us
to send ours back through the April night.

Lost Cities

ond ic hean þonan
wod ... seledreorig
and I went from there sick for home—

—"The Wanderer"

What thou love'st well remains

—Ezra Pound, Canto LXXXI

Understories

This is a party that doesn't love us.
—Tomas Tranströmer

Here I am in the Faculty Club, half an hour early
for E.'s retirement party.
The photographs at the entrance are mostly of people I never knew,
all taken twenty-five, thirty, forty years ago.
They were so now, and now they're then.
Everyone laughing, drinking, dancing—no one anxious as I feel.

At the bar I greet former colleagues as they drift in, keeping it light.
I congratulate E., splendid in a white jacket, on his retirement.
He's balder, but otherwise almost the same as in 1980,
except he's with a handsome young black man
who turns out to be his partner.

There's G., in sparkly black—she's pregnant! And D. in black and
white. She gives a polished tribute to E.'s professorial perfections—so
much I didn't know, but I recognize his jackets. So much I didn't
know—all the dinners, conversations, plots, and schemes.

What of the colleagues who aren't here?
Did someone vow to destroy them as D. did me?

And yet (said Sherlock Holmes) *I live and keep bees on the South Downs.*
I'm living, but it's still a party that doesn't love me.

And I'd need Sherlock Holmes to tell me all the understories.

Planet of the Lost Things

Phantom Books

I always thought I'd been careful of my books,
knew they might vanish.
But there are still some I reach for that are
nowhere in the present.
The Professor and the Mermaid,
lovely story of a young man studying classics one hot Sicilian summer,
a mermaid, supple as a sea otter, long blonde hair, a classic come to life,
speaking Greek, passionate, playful, a dream lover,
who stays till the weather turns and the mermaids go back to sea.
I've bought it twice, lent it twice, it's gone.
And *The Woodlanders*, my favourite Hardy— Giles Winterborne,
loved well in life and after. What I remember:
damp southern English air, tragic and intense.
I can walk into it, even now.
What was I thinking when I packed my books?
Did I think I was done with Keats?
Or German grammar?
If I could mislay the books I loved,
what about things I treasured less?

Phantom Stores

At sixty-eight I walk through vanished worlds,
through streets irrevocably changed
I'm still turning corners to failed coffee shops,

dreaming egg and anchovy sandwiches,
looking forward to browsing for antiques
in stores now sushi places or Runners' Choice.

I miss Paradiso, green and leafy
in whitest winter.
If Mrs. Dalloway had bought flowers in Kingston,
she'd have bought them here:
wondrous lilies, purple alliums, green bells of Ireland,
perfect for any party.
And Sultan's Bazaar—
exotic rugs and tablecloths, onyx goblets.
Alison presiding high-priestesslike over hand-carved
furniture and water-pipes she'd shepherded
from souks and villages.
I didn't lose these stores, but still, they're gone.

Phantom Clothes

It's the clothes I miss most,
the clothes and the body that wore them.
That kicky sixties dress,
swirling black and white
like a zebra on pot—
I wore it with yellow stockings,
blue earrings, yellow hat.
It probably wouldn't have lasted
fifty years. I miss it
and that long black sweater,
that felt like sliding inside a licorice stick—

was I careless enough
to let moths at it? Or did I give it away
because an astrologer told me
wearing black let in the dark?
I saved a blue silk suit,
one that doesn't date.
It's hanging out in the back of my closet.
I never wear it.
The Suttles and Seawinds jacket, golds and purples,
magnificent—waiting for me
with those gold drop earrings, too soon vanished friends,
the amber necklace which slipped off
two months before I removed my wedding ring forever
on the planet of the lost things.

A Walk Among the Dead

I Bay Street

Walking along Bay Street, half present,
eyes soaring to the tops of massive towers,
half in the past—when did they grow so high?
I hardly recognize the small Victorian city
I came to years ago under its endless sky.

Back then, these streets were mine,
mine and my friends'. Don, Andrew,
Mike Dixon, Millar MacLure. I envy
Odysseus pouring out blood for his ghosts
so they could speak. I'd do that if I could—
descend, find them, talk one final time.

Don, my almost brother,
what would you say if you were walking here?
I imagine you as I pull open the door
to the new opera house—light, complex—
settling into its space as if it had always been—
you'd love it. I find my seat, anticipate
Gluck's *Orfeo ed Euridice*—
pull your spirit into the empty seat beside me.

II Labour Day Weekend, 1965

I tumble from the bus, blear-eyed

after an all-night ride, uneasy sleep,
into the brightness of an unfamiliar city.
I call the Y on Woodlawn, drop my stuff,
search out the university and buy
three volumes of Euripides to see me
through a weekend when all the doors are closed.
I'm not ready for walks among the dead:
I'm twenty-one. My first step toward
claiming my own life, arriving alone,
where I know no one, reading Euripides
under ancient trees.

I'm gripped by the story of Alcestis, who died
in place of her husband Admetus, and Heracles

who fought death to bring her back.
The Bacchae—appearance of the new god Dionysus,
start of a new age, like now, the Sixties!
 I don't like Pentheus, rigid old ruler,
almost think he deserves his fate (though still,
I'm horrified—torn to death by his mother and other Maenads).
I don't think till later: I've been torn to pieces too,
my mother's words—not because I can't renounce
Apollo—can't you honour both?—but because I'm
too imperfect to fulfill my life. Maybe too because
my mother has some despair about her own.
So here I am, alone, shredded, looking for home.

By Tuesday, I've read all of Euripides and things are open.
I go back to campus, large, sprawling, a place with traditions
I have yet to learn. No signs anywhere. When I ask where to go,
people can't believe I wouldn't know.

III Alchemy

By the next summer, I start to realize ideas are in the air.
My Spenser professor, Millar MacLure, talks of alchemy
in *The Fairie Queene*, how red pulls against white, completes it;
how dark interweaves with light;
mutability shapeshifts within the broad canopy of
eternity. Alchemy, no dingy chemistry experiment, no
scam, but the true inner work of higher calling.
MacLure leads us through the immensities of Spenser,
talking of Hermes Trismegistus in an incantatory voice—
loves curious knowledge for its own sake, understands melancholy
in his bones. Talks of *The Winter's Tale*, of loss restored.
His green eyes still hold the weather of New Brunswick
and its rolling hills.
                              Much later he said *I wish I'd stayed
home and raised horses*. But if he had,
how would I have understood that education is
the door to mysteries?

By that summer, Don's become a friend. I meet
Mike and Dulcie Dixon at his party, in his small hot rooms
on Wellesley—rooms so hot Don studies in the bathtub—
Mike, dark, handsome, mischievous, puffing his pipe, says,

I've always wanted to name a journal <u>Catalyst.</u>
I wanted to start a magazine. A group gathered later
around the name. But the birth was at Don's party.
Dulcie: tiny, pretty, red-haired, valiant.
Their marriage lasted nearly fifty years.

They'd have us back for coffee after writing workshops; we'd keep
discussing around their captain's table while their cat Azma purred,
then
showed off, jumping high on kitchen shelves—writing should jump
that high. He gave his blessing to the manuscript.

I met Andrew drinking coffee in Hart House,
a book on cybernetics by his cup—
we started talking and stayed up late
many nights that fall talking alchemy
and covers—he had large ideas, drew sketches, vanished—
before the printer's deadline. Just another crisis—for the magazine,
for my comedy of errors lovelife. We found another cover.
He found another lover. I found another mismatch.
No one told me when he died. No one saved the notice in the paper.

The alchemy happened. *Catalyst* came out.
Not very good, my mother said. Too bad—
it's in the archives now. Fall, 1967: Margaret Avison,
Dennis Lee, Roy Miki, Rafael Barreto-Rivera, later
one of the Four Horsemen, Penny Chalmers, later Kemp,
now Poet Laureate of London. Mike's sonnets.

We didn't think those three years a star nursery. We didn't think

transformation, but it happened. And still goes on, loss as well as gain,
as, years later, I walk these once-familiar streets.

IV A Gathering on the Roof

Tonight I'm on the roof of my hotel,
dizzy from the drop from roof to street.
There's the bus terminal, scarcely changed—
so small. There are a few two and three story buildings
between the towers, the nostalgia district.

An ant crawls on the railing's underside,
surefooted, steady, no fear of smashing
far below.

Since I can't descend, I summon up my dead,
Don, who died of AIDS at 43,
eyes full of light that saw
right into the core of people and books.
I tell him I still miss him. I don't need him to tell me
what I owe him: keeping the faith, carrying the spirit
of the Sixties, trying to speak true.

MacLure died of a stroke, not young,
not venerably old. I hope he's spending
some of his afterlife with that great Queen,
with Spenser, in the Renaissance, since after death
all ages blend. I want to tell him, *I tried to teach like you.*
I hear the softness of his voice,
water and rolling fields. *Better, I hope.*

No, I say, *Not as well, but I kept trying.*
Mike—I know he's waiting for Dulcie,
but he'd take the time to greet me.
He lived to retire, a professor loved and revered.
I can see his lopsided smile, a Gemini after all:
everything's funny but serious too,
Andrew—his spirit belongs to others more than me.
I'd like another conversation,
I'd ask about that cover I never saw!
hope he's manifesting houses in the clouds.

I'd tell them I'm still trying to transform,
haven't made it yet to gold.

Red hibiscus blossoms spectral in the dark.
Lots of space between these towers for spirits to come
and vanish back into the night.

The Exeter Book

Father Shook, white-haired,
kind-mannered, orderly,
living in the starlight of true scholars,
led us through *The Exeter Book.*
Heavy on saints' lives
but also The Phoenix! The Wife's
Lament! Deor! The Wanderer!
Riddles! Must have been copied out
by a monk with a fine, twinkling eye.
Priests were a mystery to me then,
as was Anglo-Saxon, that
poetry of the centuries when
"nothing happened" (they said in
high school).
Poetry full of sea and sky, truth and loss.
Heroic resolve to fight until God granted
death or glory.

In the page between The Panther and
The Whale I find a note from Dan Pagnucco:
Keep this up and you'll be a BROKEN woman
also a four-leaf clover from Queen's Park.
I taught *Beowulf* for seven years; he
took off his clothes in a Paris taxi.

Looking back at that vanished time,
at a language rusted from disuse,
thinking of Father Shook and my
scattered classmates—they'd all be older
than he was then—I feel like a
last survivor—but I could never chant a lament so
wide-skied, so powerful, so lasting
as those poems we read.

Map of Florence, 1480

Places hold memory.
—Helen Humphreys

I could enter this map:
sun-kissed biscuit-coloured houses
under joyous red tile roofs,
still there after five hundred years.
The Duomo, the Baptistery,
the Giotto campanile, the Uffizi,
Santa Maria Novella—a couple streets
south of Santa Croce and east of the Bargello
I'd find the best gelato in Firenze—
jewel-toned raspberry, mango,
arancia, melone, fragola.

The shock of seeing the Arno
five hundred years younger,
not the sullen brown ribbon I remember
but swirling blue, live with fish,
surging with Renaissance energy toward Pisa
and the sea. Men standing on the banks,
ready to plunge into cool; boats cresting river swells,
fishermen attentive to stretched net.

Landscape of genius: green hills,
city walled, not sprawling, dusty as today.

We the inheritors walk where Dante walked,
Giotto, Masaccio, Botticelli, Brunelleschi.
The streets embrace us,
their stones full of stories.

Lost City

For me, New York is still *the* city—
Pete Seeger at Carnegie Hall,
the Pro Musica at the Cloisters,
Coltrane at the Fillmore.
Grand Central's still *the* station,
hub to anywhere,
secret whispering gallery
outside the Oyster Bar
long-vanished.
Central Park's *the* park
around *the* museum, the Met—
sprawled couples reading
The Sunday New York Times—

Art intertwined with life—
turn a corner, find a Greek vase
or a Nolde or the Guggenheim or Frick.
The New York Public Library
(*the place for you and the place for me*
sang the skipping school girls)
had everything, even *The Waste Land* manuscript.
Under the high ceilings,
the air breathed books.

II

When my mother died,

I knew I'd lost New York.
I walked down Madison Avenue,
numb, alone, past raspberry silk
dresses, didn't try them on.
I returned to my parents' apartment,
paid the babysitter, took Alan in my arms,
sang—another start on the long
journey of mothering.

I didn't lose it all at once. Visits
grew shorter as
light after light went out
in the apartments of my parents' friends.
I still visited Rembrandt's self-portrait
and Holbein's Sir Thomas More at the Frick,
Van Gogh's Starry Night, Matisse's Red Studio
at the Modern,
wondered if I should have stayed.
But Pluto and Uranus conjunct my sun meant
change or die.

Even this morning, cheered by the mock-orange and pink roses
against grey stone, red brick, stately maples stretching into summer
on this quiet street, I miss it.

A quiet exile, not political, tormented, like Ovid's,
Dante's, Mandelstam's (*silence, exile, cunning,*
said Joyce).
                    But still, an exile.

My Parents' Friends

I Arthur

If I went back to New York, I'd know just where to find them.
Arthur in his eyrie overlooking the Whitney,
his roof garden planted with apples and quince, roses and hostas,
something always blooming, something fruiting.
His walls covered with paintings by friends—the Alice Neels
I loved—flowers on the table, portrait of her son.
His display cases showed his collections of pre-Columbian temples,
smooth stone squares or rectangles with columns in them
small enough to fit in a hand. Spaces between like tiny doors,
maybe to guide souls out and in.
I don't know what they are, but I like them, Arthur would say,
his voice low, slow, considered.
His other collection: Peruvian hats, brightly coloured and patterned,
reds, greens, yellows, checks and steps.
Arthur himself, craggy, formidable, steady.

He took the best pictures of my mother, the only
ones that showed her happy, in that sunlit time after the war.
Her face was softer; she looked pleased. I think she was pregnant
then with my lost brother or sister, the cells scraped away as fall
dwindled into winter.

In age, after his strokes, light shone through him, grey
light through winter trees. He was still working on walking,
recovering lost ground again and again. This time the body
had other ideas.

II Frances

Frances went to kindergarten with my father in 1905.
I'd find her on East 79th between Lex and Third,
her south-facing apartment, uncluttered, bright.
A low bookcase near the door housed sets of Shakespeare;
on the top shelf about waist-high, her big book of Greece,
the pictures her oracle—she'd choose one for the day:
Delphi for good days, broken columns on the ground for bad.

Frances, small-boned, white haired, passionate, loyal,
learned Greek at 55, read Homer, travelled the landscape of the *Odyssey*.
Head on the same path as heart, no trivial pursuits.
She went to Shakespeare when she could,
Hamlet her favourite—*of course I'm in love with Hamlet.*

Frances spoke in winged words—memorable after fifty years.
But I also remember my mother telling me that Frances showed her
poems to a professor who criticized it so sharply
she never wrote again. What happens to a writer who doesn't write?
What would she have written if she'd written?
She read passionately, deeply; looked at art with gusto;
believed anything was possible and worked to make it happen
for her daughter, her grandkids, her friends.
At 77, her well-used heart gave out when she was with her
much-loved grandson Tony—she told him she was dying,
told him what to do and (probably) that he and his sister
and their mother were the joys of her life,
though that wasn't in my mother's version.

III Teddy

I'd find her on East 84th her apartment
sparer than Frances', less bookish.
Frances dressed because she had to—
but Teddy liked bright colours—orange, turquoise, gold.
Teddy's not prepared for old age, Frances said.
I wasn't sure, but now I think spirit, gallantry,
swimming, work and friends
filled her life well, even in age—love too—but
my mother didn't tell me till after Teddy died.
Teddy was dark, vivid, wise, looked the way I'd like to if I'd spent
more time swimming; less, reading.
My mother's closest friend—when I was young, we'd visit her mother's
country house with its good view of Greylock, pick raspberries,
swim, catch frogs in the pond they'd made, walk through woods.
Teddy's specialty: practical magic, quite enough for aging.

As they grew older, Frances would ask, *How does your mother seem?*
She's been a prisoner in that apartment. How is Teddy?
My mother would ask, *Was Frances smoking? Did she ask you to go*
for cigarettes? Under the worry, deep friendship.

IV Max

An army friend of Arthur and my father, of Alice Neel,
and later, of my mother. Lived on an army pension in a basement
flat on East 13th. Paint peeling, layers of rose, cream, blue—
Looks like Naples Max said, pleased.
He'd been a friend of Stein and Toklas, baptized by
Teilhard de Chardin. Arthritis gnarled his hands and feet;

cataracts blurred his eyes. Still he kept writing novels
of faith and myth and violence. My parents thought
Max had a tragic life, a writer's life,
the kind most likely to survive mere death, I thought.
When his novels reappeared, he'd live again.

V Post-Script

I thought they'd be there forever, like Central Park,
New York-y, unpretentious lives.

The way's still in my feet—those apartments,
those older streets, but the city, and the times
have changed, and I don't know where to find
the secret door.

Ovid's Exile

I Last Night in Rome

December. Packing done. Ship waiting.
Ovid embraces his beloved wife,
turns toward the door, returns,
embraces her again. Sets his feet
forward—turns once more
for the last time—tries to memorize
her touch, her kiss, sees
the moon over the courtyard.
Then, legs carrying him against
his heart's wishes, he leaves, step
by step, distance irrevocable.

II Voyage

Wind. Rain. Storms so dreadful
he barely feels the rail,
wonders if the captain can hold the wheel.
Rain pelts inside his mouth, nose.
The ship so wave-tossed he fears
exile might end right here,
almost wishes it, except for the grief
his death would cause his wife.
Not that his wishes count.
It's all up to the captain and the weather.
In this wreck of his life, he thanks the gods
for one last good decision—to spare his wife
the terrors of the ship's tilting, shuddering,

plunging, assault of rain,
indignity of being guarded, dread
of being robbed. No it's a man's world,
and not the best. Thank Vesta and great Jove
she's safe at home.

III Landscapes

Though he can barely see through
cloud and rain, he knows he's plunging
past places he wrote about in his
not-quite-finished *Metamorphoses*

If it survives, it will have to go on,
unrevised, without him.
More often than poets wish,
art predicts life.
Was it this poem that brought him
so far from Rome and Athens?

The ship struggles through the Mediterranean,
the Aegean, past Athens, around the tip of Greece.
A second storm-tossed ship staggers north,
through the Hellespont, where Helle tumbled off
the golden ram and died, north to Scythia,
home of Getae and fierce Sarmatians,
to Tomis, named for Medea's cutting up
her brother and hurling the pieces one by one
into the sea so that her pursuing father would have

to stop, gather them. Even the myths are gloomy.
Finally, the ship spits him out at the edge of empire,
on the Black Sea's sinister shore.

IV First Days

He knew he'd be lonely, knew
it was a metamorphosis
too dark for myth. He didn't expect
frigid wind roaring down from the North
forcing its way into his hut, through
too-thin clothes—didn't expect to be issued
armor for protection when the Sarmatians
swooped down on horseback pounding the frozen Danube,
fierce as north wind, shooting poisoned arrows
over the walls—every roof quilled with them.
Cold so intense, his wine is ice;
he has to lick his drink.
The streets unpaved, houses rude,
ragged edge where frayed threads of empire
meet the wild. No trees,
uncouth languages—he signs
his meanings.

Mind can span distance,
as can dreams.
But waking
is heartbreak.

V Carmen et Error

Not exiled, but "relegated"—

he retains citizenship, property.
His wife, safe, lives in their home,
walks the Roman streets, visits her daughter
their grandson—he is grateful.
But wonders what ill stars presided
when that not-quite friend read bits
of *The Art of Love* (the *carmen*) to prudish Caesar,
when Ovid saw something untoward
(the *error*). The confluence spelled
disaster, brought him to this half-life.
In spring, he walks the shore of the Black Sea,
wearing armor, working out hexameters.
Still careful in his letters not to address
friends by name—doesn't want them
tarred by his disgrace.
He can still see the moon, remembers it
above the courtyard that last night,
tries to remember his wife's touch.

I don't ask for home he writes Augustus, *but only
some place milder, safer.*

VI The Days Stretch Into Years

He starts to learn Sarmatian, Gettan.
Augustus dies. Tiberius succeeds—
Ovid hopes, writes home; no recall comes.
A friend promises to work for his return—
dies before intention manifests.
Why languish here? What good
can his exile now possibly do Rome?

He writes a poem in Gettan, reads it
in a tavern to a round of cheers.
Did that lead to some of them studying Latin?
Somehow they learn what he's been
writing home, threaten to break his hands.

How can poetry do this to him again?

VII Two Thousand Years Later

Ovid's likeness stands in Ovid Square,
transplanted, unexpected elegance.
Poets who came after wrote Romanian,
uttermost outpost of Romance language.
The land's at peace—what was a porous border
now home to birds.
The emperor must have known:
to change a colony for good, beyond mere war,
send a poet.

Orpheus

All agree his music
was magic—birds, beasts,
trees, stones, shades in hell—
all listened rapt.
Even frozen Pluto melted at his songs,
agreed to release Eurydice,
if only, *if only,* Orpheus never
looked back until they'd climbed up
above, under the dome of sky.

Eurydice stumbled, unlucky feet,
cried out. Orpheus turned
to see her vanishing a second time,
heard the wisps of last good-bye.

How easy to rage against this ending,
want it changed, like Gluck did in his
heavenly opera, where love conquers all.

But in the ancient story,
loss is part of myth,
loneliness the musician's path.
The end, violent, unexpected:
Maenads, in bloody frenzy, rip
Orpheus to pieces
thinking honour to Apollo
insult to Dionysus.

Except that's not the ending either.

After death,
his severed head proclaimed:
I am the child of earth and starry heaven.
Said, *when you descend to Hades,*
walk past forgetful Lethe. Drink from the spring
of memory. These words—
foundation of the Orphic mysteries.

Even now, Orpheus invites
listeners into the truth of myth,
says, *search out your own antidotes to oblivion,*
snatch them from silence.
Life run—the story stretches on.

Tea with Cathleen

After years of chatting on the streets,
a rift in the press of urgencies.
Cathleen talks as she makes tea
in her Vermeer-grey kitchen
this quiet morning. Good light,
tall windows.

I knew her father slightly
forty years ago,
a kind professor who always said hello.
Now Cathleen tells me:
he escaped to England from Amsterdam
the last day before the Nazis
flooded in. His mother already dead.
His father, a survivor, had been a lawyer
before the war—after, a dishwasher in Chicago,
too poor to travel to Canada
to see his son; his son too poor
to travel to see him.
He went after his father died,
collected ragged clothes,
socks with gaping holes at the heels.

Touched by History

After sixty-eight years
outside looking in,
history taps me on the shoulder.
I thought I was living my life
letting my cats in and out,
walking by the lake,
grilling fish for dinner,
when suddenly history says,
It's your turn for ruin.
Why should you be exempt,
safer than millions out of work,
homeless, on the streets?
When times go bad, governments
flex their muscles, pass laws
that let them take what they want,
arrest who they want.

Irène Némirovsky, sitting on her blue
sweater in the Maie woods, leaves
wet with last night's storm, July 11, 1942,
writing *Suite Française,* that tribute to
French bourgeois life in the midst of war,
that care with cheese, fruit,
serenity of polished wood
and lace. Arrested July 13.
Killed in Auschwitz, August 17,
age thirty-nine.

In her notebook she wrote:

What lives on:
1. Our humble day-to-day lives
2. Art
3. God

Her daughter saved half-finished *Suite Française*
in a suitcase, didn't dare read it for fifty years.

Touched by history,
Irène let her spirit rise above her life.

Dark ages end; justice returns.
After disaster, legacy.

Notes

"What I Like About Poetry": "I prefer not to" is one of Bartleby's signature refusals in Herman Melville's story.

"Per Aspera ad Astra": through hardships to the stars. Lex: law; Pax, peace; Pulchram, beauty, Sanitas, cleanliness; prosperitas, prosperity; Caritas, love with an overtone of charity; Amor, love; Mediocritas, mediocrity; Veritas, truth; Timor Dei, fear of God.

"One Thing I Love About H.D."
H.D.; the poet Hilda Doolittle (1886-1961). Her husband, the poet Richard Aldington, had an affair with Dorothy Yorke, who lived in the flat upstairs. H.D. quotes him in her novel *Bid Me to Live*. *The reddest rose unfolds*: in "Red Roses for a Beggar," *Hermetic Definitions*.

"Horoscopes": these are real horoscopes (thanks, Café Astrology!), but I have never met the person attached to either of them.

"Playing Cards": The Waite Tarot deck, one of the seminal Tarot decks of the twentieth century, was envisioned by A.E. Waite, the Arthurian scholar, and drawn by Pamela Coleman Smith, first published, 1910.

"Mean Mothers": *sterreless*, without a rudder, or possibly, star.

"Summer's Children and Their Mother": *Summer's Children* is a book of photographs and some text by Barbara Morgan (Morgan & Morgan, 1951). Doris's words appear p. 119.

"Miracles": This poem is for Hollay Ghadery in celebration of the birth of her first child.

"Time Travel": *Memory is a kind/ of accomplishment,* see William Carlos Williams, "The Descent," *Pictures from Brueghel* (New Directions), 73.

"Leaping Over Fragments": H.D.'s weaving of Sappho's words, "The Wise Sappho," *Notes on Thought & Vision* (City Lights Books, San Francisco, 1982), 63. Anne Carson's translation of Sappho's poetry, *If Not, Winter* shows how fragmentary Sappho's texts often are. In some cases there are only dative plural endings or other particles, definitely a problem for translators.

"Last Week": Sylvia Plath died Feb. 11, 1963. The italicized lines are all from her late poems.

"Paterson Ewen": This poem is for Karen Dempster, not because of the content, but with thanks for braving snarled Toronto traffic and discovering what seemed the last available parking space within walking distance of the Art Gallery of Ontario so that I could return to the Paterson Ewen show there and finish the poem.

"Still Life With Music": *se Florindo è fedele…* (if Florindo is faithful, I'll fall in love). This poem is for Marie Anderson, my wonderful teacher who brought me back to singing.

"*Io ho sofferto molto*": I've suffered greatly.

"Planet of the Lost Things": Thanks to Mark Strand for this evocative title.

"A Walk Among the Dead": Thanks to Ruth Roach Pierson for

inviting me to *Orfeo ed Euridice* and for providing living company. This opera also inspired my Orpheus poem.

"The Exeter Book": The longest and most varied of the four great Anglo-Saxon poetry manuscripts.

"Map of Florence, 1480": This map was blown up across a wall of the Art Gallery of Ontario during the Early Renaissance Exhibit, making it easy to (almost) enter.

"Ovid's Exile": I read Ovid's last writings in David Slavitt's fine translation, *Ovid's Poetry of Exile* (Johns Hopkins, 1989). Ovid says he was exiled for *carmen* (a song or poem) and *error* (a mistake, possibly inadvertently seeing something he shouldn't have). Thanks to Norm Sibum who suggested that I read Ovid's poems of exile.

Acknowledgements

Many thanks

This book began in Chile in a workshop given by Barry Dempster, organized by Susan Siddeley and given in her home, Los Paronnales. Barry's reading of "Planet of the Lost Things" encouraged me to continue writing "lost things" poems until the manuscript began to gather. Also woven into the book's beginning is the memory of our group sitting outside Neruda's Santiago home, feet in the decorative pool, on a hot late afternoon in January, reading our poems out loud, homage to Neruda.

Andrée Beauchamp (Dharani), Barry and Karen Dempster, Cynthia French, Anne Hardcastle, Jason Heroux, Helen Humphreys, Tara Kainer, Laurie Lewis, Jennifer Londry, Jeanette Lynes, Kath MacLean, Susan Olding, Gail Scala and Sheila Stewart all provided friendship, support and encouragement.

Cynthia French, Katerina Fretwell, Carol Gall, Phil Hall, Rebecca Luce-Kapler and Peter Sims read early versions of the poems and made excellent suggestions. Special thanks to Rebecca for reading and editing the entire manuscript carefully and perceptively.

Great gratitude to the Saskatchewan Writers' Guild and St. Peter's Abbey, Muenster, Saskatchewan for two wonderful retreats where several of these poems were written.

Great gratitude also to my editor and publisher at Inanna Publications, Luciana Ricciutelli, for her belief in my poetry and her work seeing it through press.

My son Alan Clark brightens my dailiness. I also thank him for his beautiful magnolia picture on the cover of this book, for the author picture, and for the photographs that inspired several of the poems.

My greatest thanks to Helen Humphreys, who read the manuscript twice, separated the living words from the listless and encouraged me to go forward with what remained. Also, thanks, Helen, for finding the title.

Equally great thanks to Barry Dempster, who gave the manuscript a very thorough final edit before it went to press. And thanks to both for their amazing writing which keeps me reaching.

Some of these poems have been published previously in journals and anthologies:

"Disturbing the Universe" in *Shy: An Anthology*, ed. Rona Altrows and Naomi Lewis (University of Alberta Press).

"Horoscopes" in *The Literary Review of Canada*.

"Planet of the Lost Things" and "Summer's Children and Their Mother" were finalists for the Descant/Winston Collins Prize in 2011 and 2013.

"Phantom Stores" ("Planet of the Lost Things") in *Poetry from Planet Earth*, ed. Yvonne Blomer and Cynthia Woodman Kerkham (Leaf Press).

"Miracles" in the *Queen's Feminist Review*.

"Leaping Over Fragments" in *Poet to Poet Anthology*, ed. Julia Roorda and Elana Wolff (Guernica).

"*Io ho sofferto molto*" in *The Antigonish Review.*

"Vibration" in *That Not Forgotten*, ed. Bruce Kauffman (Hidden Brook Press).

"New Year's Day, 2013" in *Remembering Colin Bernhardt*, ed. Michael Bawtree (Like No Other Press).

"Inheritance" in *Canadian Woman Studies/les cahiers de la femme.*

"La règle du jeu" is forthcoming in *I Found It at the Movies*, ed. Ruth Roach Pierson (Guernica).

"Raindrops Falling on Magnolia Buds" is forthcoming in the *Queen's Feminist Review.*

Many thanks to the editors of these journals and anthologies.

Elizabeth Greene has published two previous collections of poetry, *The Iron Shoes* (2007) and *Moving* (2010). She edited and contributed to *We Who Can Fly: Poems, Essays and Memories in Honour of Adele Wiseman* (1997), which won the Betty and Morris Aaron Prize for Best Scholarship on a Canadian Subject, 1998. She has edited/co-edited four other books, including *Kingston Poets' Gallery* (2006), *The Window of Dreams: New Canadian Writing for Children* with Mary Alice Downie and M.-A. Thompson (1986); *On the Threshold: Writing Toward the Year 2000* with Foxglove Collective, T. Anne Archer, Mary Cavanagh, Tara Kainer, Janice Kirk (1999); and *Common Magic: The Book of the New*, with Danielle Gugler (2008). Her poetry and fiction have also been published in journals and magazines across North America. Her poetry was a finalist for Descant/Winston Collins Prize for Best Canadian Poem, 2011, 2013. She lives in Kingston with her son and three cats.